D1330811

OLD MAPS AND NEW
SELECTED POEMS

OLD MAPS AND NEW

SELECTED POEMS

By

Norman MacCaig

1978

THE HOGARTH PRESS

LONDON

Published by
The Hogarth Press Ltd
40 William IV Street
London WC2N 4DG

*

Clarke, Irwin & Co Ltd
Toronto

*The publisher acknowledges the financial
assistance of The Scottish Arts Council in
the publication of this volume.*

British Library Cataloguing in Publication Data

MacCaig, Norman
  Old maps and new.
  I. Title
  821'.9'12   PR6025.A1628
  ISBN 0-7012-0450-8

Printed in Great Britain by
Redwood Burn Ltd
Trowbridge and London

Contents

Poems from
RIDING LIGHTS

SUMMER FARM

Straws like tame lightnings lie about the grass
And hang zigzag on hedges. Green as glass
The water in the horse-trough shines.
Nine ducks go wobbling by in two straight lines.

A hen stares at nothing with one eye,
Then picks it up. Out of an empty sky
A swallow falls and, flickering through
The barn, dives up again into the dizzy blue.

I lie, not thinking, in the cool, soft grass,
Afraid of where a thought might take me — as
This grasshopper with plated face
Unfolds his legs and finds himself a space.

Self under self, a pile of selves I stand
Threaded on time, and with metaphysic hand
Lift the farm like a lid and see
Farm within farm, and in the centre, me.

YOU WENT AWAY

Suddenly, in my world of you,
You created time.
I walked about in its bitter lanes
Looking for whom I'd lost, afraid to go home.

You stole yourself and gave me this
Torturer for my friend
Who shows me gardens rotting in air
And tells me what I no longer understand.

The birds sing still in the apple trees,
But not in mine. I hear
Only the clock whose wintry strokes
Say, 'Now is now', the same lie over and over.

If I could kill this poem, sticking
My thin pen through its throat,
It would stand crying by your bed
And haunt your cruelty every empty night.

HARPSICHORD PLAYING BACH

Translation, not transfiguration, of
The old conspiracy of space and time
Makes me conspirator too, huddling love
In my bosom like a bomb that will explode
A clock's precise and rigmaroling chime
And make a centre of the straightest road.

For space and time are those two clowns whose act
Seems all disruption. From sentimental rose
They squirt sad ink. They're the soprano's cracked
Most lamentable top note. Their stick brings down
The Hero from his nobility on his nose.
They are the itch beneath the royal crown.

Or they shake your hand and leave a death in it.
The world sits down — they pull the chair away.
On a bare hook they hang the Infinite
For the fisherman to grieve for. It's they who dowse
The lights at the quick crisis of the play.
They raise the rafters and bring down the house.

This loving music from their non-sense makes
An architecture of disruption and
Deploys a meaning in the air that shakes
The clock world off and lets the other in
Where atmospheres of meaning lead their grand
Galaxies through even a human skin.

The understanding and the loving are,
Of course, the same. Even the clock can chime
Sensibly with these notes. Six to the bar
The infinities accumulate; and I,
Drunk with the clarity of space and time,
Forget their fooling under the clownish sky.

SWIMMING LIZARD

He swam through the cool loch water
As though not knowing whether he slanted down
Or up to the brightness. Swimming was all he did.

The tiny monster, the alligator
A finger long, swam unhurried through the brown;
Each eye glittered under its heavy lid.

This was his witness and his protest,
To swim unhurried; for an unknown Cause
He twinkled his brief text through the brown and still.

And I, like it, too big to be noticed,
Hung over him in pity, and my help, too, was
No reaching hand, but a loving and helpless will.

DOUBLE LIFE

This wind from Fife has cruel fingers, scooping
The heat from streets with salty finger-tips
Crusted with frost; and all Midlothian,
Stubborn against what heeled the sides of ships
Off from the Isle of May, stiffens its drooping
Branches to the south. Each man
And woman put their winter masks on, set
In a stony flinch, and only children can
Light with a scream an autumn fire that says
With the quick crackle of its smoky blaze,
'Summer's to burn and it's October yet'.

My Water of Leith runs through a double city;
My city is threaded by a complex stream.
A matter of regret. If these cold stones
Could be stones only, and this watery gleam
Within the chasms of tenements and the pretty
Boskage of Dean could echo the groans
Of cart-wheeled bridges with only water's voice,
October would be just October. The bones
Of rattling winter would still lie underground,
Summer be less than ghost, I be unbound
From all the choking folderols of choice.

A loss of miracles — or an exchange
Of one sort for another. When the trams
Lower themselves like bugs on a branch down
The elbow of the Mound, they'd point the diagrams
Buckled between the New Town and the range
Of the craggy Old: that's all. A noun
Would so usurp all grammar no doing word
Could rob his money-bags or clap a crown
On his turned head, and all at last would be
Existence without category — free
From demonstration except as hill or bird.

And then no double-going stream would sing
Counties and books in the symbolic air,
Trundling my forty years to the Port of Leith.
But now, look around, my history's everywhere
And I'm my own environment. I cling
Like a cold limpet underneath
Each sinking stone and am the changing sea.
I die each dying minute and bequeath
Myself to all Octobers and to this
Damned flinty wind that with a scraping kiss
Howls that I'm winter, coming home to me.

COUNTRY HOUSE

Ruin creeps round the house, his wet hand fumbles
And smears the windows with weeds; he shakes from
   the hollow
And coughing pines a rain of acid — invisible
As the wild cat skulking above the craggy hill.

He roars, and one says, 'The burn's come down in spate'.
He sets the dogs barking, and goes by,
Swinging an axe and whistling, to the cottage below.
He taps on the door; there's a letter come for you.

Last night the birds perched under water; smoke
Hung flattened under fathoms of sodden air;
The roof, like a limpet, glistened; the lighted window
Was jelly-red, an anemone in flower.

But what does ruin care? We'll say tomorrow,
'Summer's come back'; he'll push hot grasses in
Between the stones, he'll file with a gay flame
The doorpost that your shoulder's leaning on.

Your thoughts come through the crippled gate, along
By the rheumatic fences to the door
With love to put in jugs in the smiling window;
But it's no good; something's been here before.

Something that leaves on the disordered slates
A thumbprint of green lichen, that sprawls the rose
Over the flaking wall, that on still nights
Rushes down headlong from the freezing stars.

NO ESCAPE

Bury my name in the ground and watch it grow.
The dead words fluttering from your mouth can waft
No nightmare stronger than this simple morning
Whose art is malice and whose kindness craft.

There's no escape. The colour of a dream
Falls into nowhere from your painting hand;
And there your fingers lie as pale and pleading
As refugees lost in my foreign land.

They gesture Go, and draw me closer in.
Your nightmare tongue says Die; and I swarm over
Your desert as green trees, and birds and lions
Come through the light to drink my singing water.

FIAT

I cannot stammer thunder in your sky
Or flash white phrases there. I have no terse
Exploding passion, and cannot vilify
My dulcet world through flute-holes of a verse,
But gently speak and, gently speaking, prove
The everlastingness in which you move.

No superscription in a cloud need sign
Either my love or hate to show they are
Come from a source more terrible than mine.
And I need bow to no peremptory star:
A finger writes, and there is star — or me,
With love or hate to cloud identity.

And time's inflections cannot alter this
Most gentle truth, that fire and thunder-head
Are momentary metamorphosis
Of the most gentle word ever was said
Into what means no less of gentleness,
Being accepting being, and saying Yes.

CLIMBING SUILVEN

I nod and nod to my own shadow and thrust
A mountain down and down.
Between my feet a loch shines in the brown,
Its silver paper crinkled and edged with rust.
My lungs say No;
But down and down this treadmill hill must go.

Parishes dwindle. But my parish is
This stone, that tuft, this stone
And the cramped quarters of my flesh and bone.
I claw that tall horizon down to this;
And suddenly
My shadow jumps huge miles away from me.

DRIFTER

The long net, tasselled with corpses, came
Burning through the water, flowing up.
Dogfish following it to the surface
Turned away slowly to the deep.

The *Daffodil* squatted, slid ahead
Through the red kyle with thirty crans
Of throttled silver in her belly.
Her anchor snored amid its chains.

And memory gathered tarry splinters,
Put shadowy sparkles in her bag,
Slid up her sleeve the hills of Harris
And stole Orion and the Dog.

I sat with that cruel thief inside me;
I sat with years I did not know
Heaped on my knees. With these two treasures
I sailed home through the Gaelic sea.

EMPTY POOL

The water moves no more than I.
Only the tottering reed-tips show
Where what I love, absurd with fear
And anguish, runs away from me.

I stand still as a post. Within me
There's anguish too, there's something
    trembling . . .
What's watching me? What tries to follow
Where I have gone, with love and pity?

FALSE SUMMER

False summer's here and the canal's
Green water breathes with lovers' kisses,
And buildings deep as herons stand
In the whirlpool of their own wishes.

The buds that made our winter tender
Feel the leaf aching and begin
Its million-year-old two-inch journey
Into the parish of the sun.

But beyond the yellow light are lurking
Microbes of frost, and in the air
Are ghosts of claws that, one clear night,
Will pinch to ashes the cheated flower.

The water will be black and glassy
Against the brittle grass-stems, and
Bewildered lovers will remember
What once flew in the freezing wind.

Poems from
THE SINAI SORT

GOLDEN CALF

If all the answer's to be the Sinai sort,
The incorruptible lava of the word
Made alphabetic in a stormspout, what
Mere human vocables you've ever heard,
Poor golden calf, could overbear, I wonder,
    The magniloquence of thunder?

You're for another flame. The Moses in me
Looks with a stone face on our gaudy lives.
His fingers, scorched with godhead, point, and
    loose
An influence of categorical negatives
That makes an image of love, a trope of lover.
    Our dancing days are over.

The buckles tarnish at the thought of it.
The winecup shatters. The bragging music chokes
To the funeral silence it was awkward in.
And before the faggot of salvation smokes,
Your knees are loosed, your wreathed neck bows
    lowly
    In presence of the holy.

What's a disgruntled cloud to you or me?
Listen to my multitudes, and beam for them,
Making a plinth of this dark wilderness.
Utter such rigmaroles an apothegm,
Doing its head-stroke, drowns in such wild water
    And proves itself no matter.

Or where's the desert cat, or hunching shade
That ambles hugely in the dark outside,
Or hospitable anguish beckoning
To its foul ceremony a sorry bride
Could bear the darts struck from your hide by
    torches
    That guard our pleasure's marches?

Forty years. Small wilderness to unravel
Such an unknotted thread of wandering.
The desert is in Moses' skull, the journey
To the white thalamus whose cradling
Enfolds the foetus of the law — gestation
   Of Moses as a nation.

A chosen people, since they have no choice.
The doors are locked, the flesh-pots on the shelves,
And a long line of lamentation moves
Led by the nose through their own better selves
To buy with blood a land of milk and honey
   Where's no need for such money.

The smoke and thunder die. And here I stand
Smelling of gunpowder and holiness.
The great fire does its belly-dance and in it
You shine unharmed, not knowing what's to
      confess;
And the desert, seeing the issue grows no clearer,
   Takes one long slow step nearer.

GIFTS

You read the old Irish poet and complain
I do not offer you impossible things —
Gloves of bee's fur, cap of the wren's wings,
Goblets so clear light falls on them like a stain.
I make you the harder offer of all I can,
The good and ill that make of me this man.

I need no fancy to mark you as beautiful,
If you are beautiful. All I know is what
Darkens and brightens the sad waste of my thought
Is what makes me your wild, truth-telling fool
Who will not spoil your power by adding one
Vainglorious image to all we've said and done.

Flowers need no fantasy, stones need no dream:
And you are flower and stone. And I compel
Myself to be no more than possible,
Offering nothing that might one day seem
A measure of your failure to be true
To the greedy vanity that disfigures you.

A cloak of the finest silk in Scotland — what
Has that to do with troubled nights and days
Of sorry happiness? I had no praise
Even of your kindness, that was not bought
At such a price this bankrupt self is all
I have to give. And is that possible?

EGO

Stare at the stars, the stars say. Look at me,
Whispers the water and protests the tree;
The rose is its own exclamation and
Frost touches with an insinuating hand.
Yet they prefigure to my human mind
Categories only of a human kind.

I see a rose, that strange thing, and what's there
But a seeming something coloured on the air
With the transparencies that make up me,
Thickened to existence by my notice. Tree
And star are ways of finding out what I
Mean in a text composed of earth and sky.

What reason to believe this, any more
Than that I am myself a metaphor
That's noticed in the researches of a rose
And self-instructs a star? Time only knows
Creation's mad cross-purposes and will
Destroy the evidence to keep them secret still.

POEM FOR A GOODBYE

When you go through
My absence, which is all of you,
And clouds, or suns, no more can be my sky,
My one dissembling will be all —
The inclusive lie
Of being this voice, this look, these few feet tall.

The elements which
Made me from our encounter rich
Cannot be uncreated; there is no
Chaos whose informality
Can cancel, so,
The ritual of your presence, even gone away.

You, then and I
Will masquerade a lie,
Diminishing ourselves to be what can
Seem one without the other, while
A greater man,
In hiding, lies behind this look, this smile.

It's he who will
Across sad oceans meet you still,
Startling your carelessness with what once was.
His voice from this past hour will speak,
Cancelling Time's laws:
In the world's presence his hand will touch your cheek.

Foreign can be
Only that sound to you and me.
There is no thought that in its dying goes
Through such a region we do not
In it compose
Each other's selves, each in the other's thought.

You leave behind
More than I was, and with a kind
Of sad prevarication take with you
More than I'll be till that day when
Nothing's to do
But say, 'At last', and we are home again.

EXPLORER

He went no further than he could not go.
Holding the waver of light in his green hand
He disappeared beyond the impossible. No
Word could befriend him in that friendless land.

Then the impossible grew its usual fruits.
The monsters withdrew beyond his ring of light.
We found him talking to us — the old disputes;
For we had been waiting for him, all the night.

And so we met ourselves again. And so
Once more we were one of him; until one day
Wanting to meet us, he prepared to go
Further impossibilities away.

Poems from
A COMMON GRACE

GOAT

The goat, with amber dumb-bells in his eyes,
The blasé lecher, inquisitive as sin,
White sarcasm walking, proof against surprise,

The nothing like him goat, goat-in-itself,
Idea of goatishness made flesh, pure essence
In idle masquerade on a rocky shelf —

Hangs upside down from lushest grass to twitch
A shrivelled blade from the cliff's barren chest,
And holds the grass well lost; the narrowest niche

Is frame for the devil's face; the steepest thatch
Of barn or byre is pavement to his foot;
The last, loved rose a prisoner to his snatch;

And the man in his man-ness, passing, feels suddenly
Hypocrite found out, hearing behind him that
Vulgar vibrato, thin derisive me-eh.

FEEDING DUCKS

One duck stood on my toes.
The others made watery rushes after bread
Thrown by my momentary hand; instead,
She stood duck-still and got far more than those.

An invisible drone boomed by
With a beetle in it; the neighbour's yearning bull
Bugled across five fields. And an evening full
Of other evenings quietly began to die.

And my everlasting hand
Dropped on my hypocrite duck her grace of bread.
And I thought, 'The first to be fattened, the first to be
    dead',
Till my gestures enlarged, wide over the darkening land.

HALF-BUILT BOAT IN A HAYFIELD

A cradle, at a distance, of a kind:
Or, making midget its neat pastoral scene.,
A carcass rotted and its bones picked clean.

Rye-grass was silk and sea, whose rippling was
Too suave to rock it. Solid in the sun,
Its stiff ribs ached for voyages not begun.

The gathering word was not completed yet.
The litter of its own genesis lay around,
Sunk in the bearded sea, or on the ground.

As though evolving brilliances could show
In their first utterances what would end as one
Continuous proclamation of a sun.

Only when these clawed timbers could enclose
Their own completing darkness would they be
Phoenixed from It and phoenixed into She.

And fit then as such noticing reveals,
To split her first wave open and explore
The many ways that all lead to one shore.

NUDE IN A FOUNTAIN

Clip-clop go water-drops and bridles ring —
Or, visually, a gauze of water, blown
About and falling and blown about, discloses
Pudicity herself in shameless stone,
In an unlikely world of shells and roses.

On shaven grass a summer's litter lies
Of paper bags and people. One o'clock
Booms on the leaves with which the trees are quilted
And wades away through air, making it rock
On flowerbeds that have blazed and dazed and wilted.

Light perches, preening, on the handle of a pram
And gasps on paths and runs along a rail
And whitely, brightly in a soft diffusion
Veils and unveils the naked figure, pale
As marble in her stone and stilled confusion.

And nothing moves except one dog that runs,
A red rag in a black rag, round and round
And that long helmet-plume of water waving,
In which the four elements, hoisted from the ground,
Become this grace, the form of their enslaving.

Meeting and marrying in the midmost air
Is mineral assurance of them all;
White doldrum on blue sky; a pose of meaning
Whose pose is what is explicit; a miracle
Made, and made bearable, by the water's screening.

The drops sigh, singing, and, still sighing, sing
Gently a leaning song. She makes no sound.
They veil her, not with shadows, but with brightness;
Till, gleam within a glitter, they expound
What a tall shadow is when it is whiteness.

A perpetual modification of itself
Going on around her is her; her hand is curled
Round more than a stone breast; and she discloses
The more than likely in an unlikely world
Of dogs and people and stone shells and roses.

FISHING THE BALVAIG

It is like being divided, stood on stumps
On a layer of water scarcely thicker than light
That parallels away to show it's water all right.

While underneath two sawn-off waders walk
Surprisingly to one's wishes — as though no man
Moved lumpishly, so, but a sort of Caliban.

The eel that tries to screw his ignorant head
Under an instep thinks the same; and goes
Like a tape of water going where the water flows.

Collecting images by redounding them,
The stream is leafed, sunned, skied and full of shade;
Pot-holed with beer and shallowed with lemonade.

But in the glides is this thicker sort of light.
It blurs no freckled pebble or nervous weed,
Whose colours quicken as it slacks its speed.

As though water and light were mistranslations of
A vivifying influence they both use
To make a thing more thing and old news, news.

Which all the world is, wheeling round this odd
Divided figure, who forgets to pass
Through water that looks like the word isinglass.

STANDING IN MY IDEAS

Never did Nature, that vogue-mistress, give
An image from her slants and sighs and silks
Or make a figure out of froth and stone
That would not blush as your alternative,
— Though, trapped in a net of kins, a web of ilks,
The gorgeous rose is sibling to the bone.

You stand entrancing in my trance of woods,
Superlatively you, and bole and bough
Surrender Ariels rotting in their rind.
The dropped cone hiccups, the cherry branch intrudes.
And with such grace you breathe what, I allow,
Is foxglove vapours hazing in my mind.

Such elegant composure I suspect
Because I love it, and my loving charms
Environment from you. And, being wise
In my suspicions, can it be I detect
Something of innocent ivy in your arms?
Something of nightshade in those lucid eyes?

TWO WAYS OF IT

The duller legends are what you live in,
The girl who knew a man who once saw Helen
Or heard a hero howling in his pride.
I, knowing you, live in a larger one —
Where, all the same, no topless tower has fallen
Nor good man gone to Hell before he died.

You are no Helen, walking parapets
And dazing wisdom with another beauty
That made hard men talk soft of goddesses
And feel death blooming in their violent wits
With such seduction that they asked no pity —
Till death came whistling in and loosed their knees.

For not death blooms but ordinariness;
And worlds and wits wake to a mundane glory
That, being its source, you can know nothing of.
This is the largest legend, that need not stress
A more than human distance or be fiery
With a god's grace that kills to keep its love.

Even a leaf, its own shape in the air,
Achieves its mystery not by being symbol
Or ominous of anything but what it is,
Such is the decent clarity you bear
For the world to be in. Everything is humble,
Not humbled, in its own lucidities.

No need to wander the dark lanes of Hell
Or be translated to a monumental
Sprinkle of stars, to mark our history:
But doucely, in your fashion, I will kill
Nothing but Time (until that final battle
When you and legends fade away from me).

To enrich the leaf and be enriched by it
And to be, both, your natural celebration,
Stating, by selves, what Time cannot outface . . .
A legend, this, with no curmudgeon plot
To make a martyr of a slave to passion —
Who am no slave, but freeman of your grace.

SPATE IN WINTER MIDNIGHT

The streams fall down and through the darkness bear
Such wild and shaking hair.
Such looks beyond a cool surmise.
Such lamentable uproar from night skies
As turn the owl from honey of blood and make
Great stags stand still to hear the darkness shake.

Through Troys of bracken and Babel towers of rocks
Shrinks now the looting fox.
Fearful to touch the thudding ground
And flattened to it by the mastering sound.
And roebuck stilt and leap sideways; their skin
Twitches like water on the fear within.

Black hills are slashed white with this falling grace
Whose violence buckles space
To a sheet-iron thunder. This
Is noise made universe, whose still centre is
Where the cold adder sleeps in his small bed,
Curled neatly round his neat and evil head.

CELTIC CROSS

The implicated generations made
This symbol of their lives, a stone made light
By what is carved on it.
                        The plaiting masks,
But not with involutions of a shade,
What a stone says and what a stone cross asks.

Something that is not mirrored by nor trapped
In webs of water or bag-nets of cloud;
The tangled mesh of weed
                        lets it go by.
Only men's minds could ever have unmapped
Into abstraction such a territory.

No green bay going yellow over sand
Is written on by winds to tell a tale
Of death-dishevelled gull
                        or heron, stiff
As a cruel clerk with gaunt writs in his hand
— Or even of light, that makes its depths a cliff.

Singing responses order otherwise.
The tangled generations ravelled out
In links of song whose sweet
                        strong choruses
Are these stone involutions to the eyes
Given to the ear in abstract vocables.

The stone remains, and the cross, to let us know
Their unjust, hard demands, as symbols do.
But on them twine and grow
                        beneath the dove
Serpents of wisdom whose cool statements show
Such understanding that it seems like love.

Poems from
A ROUND OF APPLAUSE

IN A LEVEL LIGHT

Sheep wander haloed, birds at their plainsong shed
Pure benedictions on water's painted glass.
The gentle worm rears up her hooded head
And weaves hot sermons under her steeple of grass.
Saints objurgate from thickets, angels bank
Over the sea: and its crisp texts unfold,
Silvering the sand's ecclesiastic gold.

Accepted in it all, one of its moods,
The human mind sits in its sense of sin,
Hacking a cross from gross beatitudes,
The price to pay warm in its purse of skin,
And sees out in that bliss, and out of its,
An angel tilt, dive into texts and float,
Working his god down his rebelling throat.

BYRE

The thatched roof rings like heaven where mice
Squeak small hosannahs all night long,
Scratching its golden pavements, skirting
The gutter's crystal river-song.

Wild kittens in the world below
Glare with one flaming eye through cracks,
Spurt in the straw, are tawny brooches
Splayed on the chests of drunken sacks.

The dimness becomes darkness as
Vast presences come mincing in,
Swagbellied Aphrodites, swinging
A silver slaver from each chin.

And all is milky, secret, female.
Angels are hushed and plain straws shine.
And kittens miaow in circles, stalking
With tail and hindleg one straight line.

JOHN QUIXOTE

Where he jogs dusty, trailing a horn of dust,
Ironic windmills signal through grey air
Their huge tall jokes and a lousy innkeeper
Spreads evil blankets, swansdown to his pelt;
Princes in pigsties scratch their scurfy crust
And heads of heathens stutter at his belt.

No lark so ravishing as to be a lark
Nor dirt so true as nourish one poor seed.
His mad eye twitches, hands grope for a deed
That would free heavenly hosts to sing and soar
Over gold acres, dancing round the Ark.
(He halts at byre-ends, snuffing the devil's spoor.)

No fat self follows him to keep him wrong.
High in his proper sun his high casque jogs
By scarps and enfilading gorges, dogs
Snarling in worlds below where wit and grace
And bestial scholars and thin priests belong.
— By tumbling in the dust he proves his case.

His chattering armour squeaks there as he sprawls
Under the laughing bellies, and his lance,
Clenched in his claw still, wavers through mischance
To point, true North, at his old target, till,
His head cocked high, he clatters off and bawls
Tremendous lovesongs to the tiny hills.

THINGS IN EACH OTHER

To fake green strokes in water, light fidgets,
A niggling fidget, and the green is there,
Born of a blue and marrying into blue
With clouds blushed pink on it from the upper air.

And water breathing upwards from itself
Sketches an island with blurred pencillings,
A phase of space, a melting out of space:
Mind does this, too, with the pure shapes of things.

Or the mind fidgets and a thought, grown green,
Born of nowhere and marrying nowhere,
Fakes a creation, that is one and goes
Into the world and makes its difference there.

A thing to be regarded: whose pure shape
Blurs in the quality of the noticing mind
And is blushed pink and makes the hard jump from
Created to creator, like human kind.

SPRAYING SHEEP

Old tufts of wool lie on the grass.
The clipping's over. But once again
The small quicksilver flock come pouring
Down from the hill towards the pen.

Dogs coax them to the roofless steading.
They bunch, plunge forward, one by one.
When half's outside and half within, they
Make a white hourglass in the sun.

The dogs run on the ruined walls,
Swinging their tongues, their minds all sheep.
The zinc bath winks, the stirrup pump
Guzzles the primrose one foot deep.

Then out they come, bounding high over
Nothing at all, and ramble on
The shining grass — not quicksilver
But golden fleeces, every one.

LIGHTHOUSE

Gorgon in greed, but not effect, it glares
A thing to life and back again.
A hill jumps forward, then it isn't there.
A tree explodes in tree shape. Flashes devour
This house's natural death — it has more than twenty
Punctual resurrections every hour.
Bad Christians think that one is more than plenty.

Bad disbelievers, too, are troubled by
Their disbelief — how weak it is;
And in the dark look for that whirling eye
Whose maniacal rigidity might swing
Them into high relief. . .The sea, too busy
Inventing its own forms, bucks by, leaving
The mind to spin, the dark brain to grow dizzy.

MIDNIGHT, LOCHINVER

Wine-coloured, Homer said, wine-dark. . .
The seaweed on the stony beach,
Flushed darker with that wine, was kilts
And beasts and carpets. . .A startled heron
Tucked in its cloud two yellow stilts.

And eiderducks were five, no, two—
No, six. A lounging fishbox raised
Its broad nose to the moon. With groans
And shouts the steep burn drowned itself;
And sighs were soft among the stones.

All quiet, all dark: excepting where
A cone of light stood on the pier
And in the circle of its scope
A hot winch huffed and puffed and gnashed
Its iron fangs and swallowed rope.

The nursing tide moved gently in.
Familiar archipelagoes
Heard her advancing, heard her speak
Things clear, though hard to understand
Whether in Gaelic or in Greek.

OUTSIDER

I watch the lush moon fatly smirking down —
Where she might go, to skirt that smouldering cloud,
Is space enough to lose your image in.

Or, turn my head, between those islands run
Sandpapering currents that would scrub the dull
Picture away in suds and slaverings.

Even this grass, glowered at with force enough,
And listened to with lusting, would usurp,
In its beanstalk way, the walking, talking thing.

I choose it should not go. I turn from these
Paltering beautiful things, in case I see
Your image fade and myself fade with it —

A dissipation into actual light:
A dissolution in pure wave: a demise
In growth of a good greenness, sappy and thick —

And think myself a foreigner in this scene,
The odd shape cramped on stone, the unbeastlike,
    clear
Of law and logos, with choices to commit. . .

Thump goes the wave then crisscross gabbles back —
As I do now till, wave to wonder at,
I come again, to tower and lurch and spill.

PURIFICATION

Winds whirl in their hooded caves
And tawny rocks are all asleep.
Easy to see the moon walk on this desert,
Easy to see her, smiling to herself.

Yesterday winds howled overhead,
Lions loped in the cruel light,
Cities crawled in the glare, and the horizon
Flickered with journeys, dreams, abandonments.

Wearing your self as though it were
The lightest of all garments, moving
As though all answers were a mode of movement,
You came and were as though to be were easy.

And now there is an end of storm,
Of rage and lust and wild horizons.
Desert is purely desert, in itself. . .
To be a desert, even, is difficult.

WATER TAP

There was this hayfield,
You remember, pale gold
If it weren't hazed
With a million clover heads.

A rope of water
Frayed down — the bucket
Hoisted up a plate
Of flashing light.

The thin road screwed
Into hills; all ended
Journeys were somewhere,
But far, far.

You laughed, by the fence;
And everything that was
Hoisting water
Suddenly spilled over.

HIGH UP ON SUILVEN

Gulfs of blue air, two lochs like spectacles,
A frog (this height) and Harris in the sky —
There are more reasons for hills
Than being steep and reaching only high.

Meeting the cliff face, the American wind
Stands up on end: chute going the wrong way.
Nine ravens play with it and
Go up and down its lift half the long day.

Reasons for them? The hill's one. . .A web like this
Has a thread that goes beyond the possible;
The old spider outside space
Runs down it — and where's raven? Or where's hill?

Poems from
MEASURES

FETCHING COWS

The black one, last as usual, swings her head
And coils a black tongue round a grass-tuft. I
Watch her soft weight come down, her split feet
    spread.

In front, the others swing and slouch; they roll
Their great Greek eyes and breathe out milky gusts
From muzzles black and shiny as wet coal.

The collie trots, bored, at my heels, then plops
Into the ditch. The sea makes a tired sound
That's always stopping though it never stops.

A haycart squats prickeared against the sky.
Hay breath and milk breath. Far out in the West
The wrecked sun founders though its colours fly.

The collie's bored. There's nothing to control. . .
The black cow is two native carriers
Bringing its belly home, slung from a pole.

ASPECTS

Clean in the light, with nothing to remember,
The fox fur shrivels, the bone beak drops apart;
Sludge on the ground, the dead deer drips his heart.

Clean in the weather, trees crack and lean over;
Mountain bows down and combs its scurfy head
To make a meadow and its own deathbed.

Clean in the moon, tides scrub away their islands,
Unpicking gulls. Whales that have learned to drown,
Ballooning up, meet navies circling down.

Clean in the mind, a new mind creeps to being,
Eating the old . . . Ancestors have no place
In such clean qualities as time and space.

SKITTLES

Fine alley this. A ball
That ought to trundle smooth on its small thunder
Has two legs, seemingly, one shorter than the other:
It hops, steps, hobbles towards the scattering fall.

Flat on my face, I stare
At my brown round toad crippling away. It hasn't
Much of my intentions left. Far off, the wizened
Bottle shapes stand; brown penguins. The ball's now
    square.

From snake to mantis to man
I stand upright and turn away. Behind me
A demolition says my fate has found me.
My lost intention has done what I once began.

NEGLECTED GRAVEYARD, LUSKENTYRE

I wade in the long grass,
Barking my shins on gravestones.
The grass overtops the dyke.
In and out of the bay hesitates the Atlantic.

A seagull stares at me hard
With a quarterdeck eye, leans forward
And shrugs into the air.
The dead rest from their journey from one wilderness to
    another.

Considering what they were,
This seems a proper disorder.
Why lay graves by rule
Like bars of a cage on the ground? To discipline the unruly?

I know a man who is
Peeped at by death. No place is
Atlantics coming in;
No time but reaches out to touch him with a cold finger.

He hears death at the door.
He knows him round every corner.
No matter where he goes
He wades in long grass, barking his shins on gravestones.

The edge of the green sea
Crumples. Bees are in clover.
I part the grasses and there —
Angus MacLeod, drowned. Mary his wife. Together.

NOT ONLY THERE

By Leader Water
In the dead mirk of night, I grasped a fencepost
And squashed a slug. All that I think I am
Struggled to break from that wet gray web in my palm.

By Leader Water
In the deadest dark of the night, under my foot
The world became rabbit. All my ancestors were
Tossed me a couple of clear feet in the air.

By Leader Water
Behind my back, in the quietest hush of the night,
An old ewe coughed. All that I think of men
Raised my hair up then stroked it down again.

HERON

It stands in water, wrapped in heron. It makes
An absolute exclusion of everything else
By disappearing in itself, yet is the presence
Of hidden pools and secret, reedy lakes.
It twirls small fish from the bright water flakes.

(Glog goes the small fish down.) With lifted head
And no shoulders at all, it periscopes round —
Steps, like an aunty, forward — gives itself shoulders
And vanishes, a shilling in a pound,
Making no sight as other things make no sound.

Until, releasing its own spring, it fills
The air with heron, finds its height and goes,
A spear between two clouds. A cliff receives it
And it is gargoyle. All around it hills
Stand in the sea; wind from a brown sail spills.

SHEEP DIPPING

The sea goes flick-flack or the light does. When
John chucks the ewe in, she splays up two wings
That beat once and are water once again.

Pushing her nose, she trots slow-motion through
The glassy green. The others beat and plunge —
If she must do it, what else is there to do?

They leap from ledges, all legs in the air
All furbelows and bulged eyes in the green
Turned suds, turned soda with the plumping there.

They haul themselves ashore. With outraged cries
They waterfall uphill, spread out and stand
Dribbling salt water into flowers' eyes.

TIRED SYMPATHY

Come sigh no closer than a sigh can do.
The wind that tramples on the house can bear
On it with no more weight than bulging air.
I can support no more in you than you.

The Christmas holly shrivels on its stem
And ghastly January is ill in the long street.
Greetings are done with. For what's left to greet?
All days are yesterdays, and we know them.

And all your sighing is last year's, until
You invent a Spring to freshen grief again
With cruel contrasts. I will listen when
My wells, like yours, rise, blink and overspill.

MOVEMENTS

Lark drives invisible pitons in the air
And hauls itself up the face of space.
Mouse stops being comma and clockworks on the floor.
Cats spill from walls. Swans undulate through clouds.
Eel drills through darkness its malignant face.

Fox, smouldering through the heather bushes, bursts
A bomb of grouse. A speck of air grows thick
And is a hornet. When a gannet dives
It's a white anchor falling. And when it lands
Umbrella heron becomes walking-stick.

I think these movements and become them, here,
In this room's stillness, none of them about,
And relish them all — until I think of where,
Thrashed by a crook, the cursive adder writes
Quick V's and Q's in the dust and rubs them out.

BY ACHMELVICH BRIDGE

Night stirs the trees
With breathings of such music that they sway,
Skirts, sleeves, tiaras, in the humming dark,
Their highborn heads tossing in disarray.

A floating owl
Unreels his silence, winding in and out
Of different darknesses. The wind takes up
And scatters a sound of water all about.

No moon need slide
Into the sky to make that water bright;
It ties its swelling self with glassy ropes;
It jumps from stones in smithereens of light.

The mosses on the wall
Plump their fat cushions up. They smell of wells,
Of under bridges and of spoons. They move
More quiveringly than the dazed rims of bells.

A broad cloud drops
A darker darkness. Turning up his stare,
Letting the world pour under him, owl goes off,
His small soft foghorn quavering through the air.

NO ACCIDENT

Walking downhill from Suilven (a fine day, for once)
I twisted a knee. Two crippling miles to walk.
Leap became lower. Bag swung from a bowed neck.
Pedant of walking learned it like a dunce.

I didn't mind so much. Suilven's a place
That gives more than a basket of trout. It opens
The space it lives in and a heaven's revealed, in glimpses.
Grace is a crippling thing. You've to pay for grace.

The heaven's an odd one, shaped like cliff and scree
No less than they are: no picnicking place, but hiding
Forevers and everywheres in every thing — including
A two-mile walk, even, and a crippled knee.

You reach it by revelation. Good works can't place
Heaven in a dead hind and a falcon going
Or on the hard truth that, if only by being
First in a lower state, you've to pay for grace.

TRUE WAYS OF KNOWING

Not an ounce excessive, not an inch too little,
Our easy reciprocations. You let me know
The way a boat would feel, if it could feel,
The intimate support of water.

The news you bring me has been news forever,
So that I understand what a stone would say
If only a stone could speak. Is it sad a grassblade
Can't know how it is lovely?

Is it sad that you can't know, except by hearsay
(My gossiping failing words) that you are the way
A water is that can clench its palm and crumple
A boat's confiding timbers?

But that's excessive, and too little. Knowing
The way a circle would describe its roundness,
We touch two selves and feel, complete and gentle,
The intimate support of being.

The way that flight would feel a bird flying
(If it could feel) is the way a space that's in
A stone that's in a water would know itself
If it had our way of knowing.

Poems from
SURROUNDINGS

GO BETWEEN

Out of a night
that felt like a grape's skin
an owl's voice shuddered.
Out of the running
blackness of a river pool
a white salmon unplugged
itself and fell back
in a smash of light.
Out of the throat of
a duck flying over,
delicate, Japanese
on the blue plate of the sky,
came a croaking grunt,
catarrhal and fat-living.
Out of your never
averted face, come
classical admonitions
of the finality of form
and the untrespassable regions
beyond it. I go
poaching there and come
back with news of
an owl's hoot, exploding
salmon and the profound eructations
from the flat nose of
a delicate duck.

Since I am your convert
and true believer, I have
to enlarge the admonitions
of your never averted face
to include these wild regions
where the lunacy of form
is normal and caricature
impossible. Am I bringing
your news to them or their news
to you? Am I evangelising

the duck or you? — For how can a man
breathe hymns to the Lord
with one lung and hymns to the devil
with the other?

FROGS

Frogs sit more solid
than anything sits. In mid-leap they are
parachutists falling
in a free fall. They die on roads
with arms across their chests and
heads high.

I love frogs that sit
like Buddha, that fall without
parachutes, that die
like Italian tenors.

Above all, I love them because,
pursued in water, they never
panic so much that they fail
to make stylish triangles
with their ballet dancer's
legs.

SOUNDS OF THE DAY

When a clatter came,
it was horses crossing the ford.
When the air creaked, it was
a lapwing seeing us off the premises
of its private marsh. A snuffling puff
ten yards from the boat was the tide blocking and
unblocking a hole in a rock.
When the black drums rolled, it was water
falling sixty feet into itself.

When the door
scraped shut, it was the end
of all the sounds there are.

You left me
beside the quietest fire in the world.

I thought I was hurt in my pride only,
forgetting that,
when you plunge your hand in freezing water,
you feel
a bangle of ice round your wrist
before the whole hand goes numb.

ASSISI

The dwarf with his hands on backwards
sat, slumped like a half-filled sack
on tiny twisted legs from which
sawdust might run,
outside the three tiers of churches built
in honour of St. Francis, brother
of the poor, talker with birds, over whom
he had the advantage
of not being dead yet.

A priest explained
how clever it was of Giotto
to make his frescoes tell stories
that would reveal to the illiterate the goodness
of God and the suffering
of His Son. I understood
the explanation and
the cleverness.

A rush of tourists, clucking contentedly,
fluttered after him as he scattered
the grain of the word. It was they who had passed
the ruined temple outside, whose eyes
wept pus, whose back was higher
than his head, whose lopsided mouth
said *Grazie* in a voice as sweet
as a child's when she speaks to her mother
or a bird's when it spoke
to St. Francis.

FLOODED MIND

When the water fell
the trees rose up again
and fish stopped being birds
among the branches.

The trees were never the same again, though,
and the birds
often regarded him
with a very fishy eye
as he walked the policies of himself,
his own keeper.

Also, he was afraid to go fishing
in case he landed a fish
with feathers that would sing
in his net.

No wonder his eyes were
noticeboards saying
Private. Keep out.

ABOVE INVERKIRKAIG

I watch, across the loch
where seatrout are leaping,
Suilven and Cul Mor, my
mountains of mountains,
looming and pachydermatous in the thin light
of a clear half moon. Something swells
in my mind, in my self, as though
I were about to be enlarged,
to enclose informations and secrets
that lie just beyond me, that I would utter
in one short, stupendous sentence, to the everlasting
benefit of mankind and landscapes and me —
a pregnant feeling that is, naturally, caused
by love.

I know, half-moon-struck as I am,
the usual miscarriage will follow. I am beyond
the reach of miracles. And am glad of it,
thinking that, if this miracle were to happen
this time, it would be as if
Suilven should monstrously
move over to Cul Mor and after
coupling through human generations
drag himself back and sit
by his own lochside, indifferently
observing on the bogs of Assynt
a litter of tiny Suilvens, each one
the dead spit of his father.

LINGUIST

If we lived in a world where bells
truly say "ding-dong" and where "moo"
is a rather neat thing
said by a cow,
I could believe you could believe
that these sounds I make in the air
and these shapes with which I blacken
white paper have some reference
to the thoughts in my mind
and the feelings in the thoughts.

As things are,
if I were to gaze in your eyes and say
"bow-wow" or "quack", you must take that to be
a despairing anthology of praises,
a concentration of all the opposites
of reticence, a capsule
of my meaning of meaning
that I can no more write down
than I could spell the sound of the sigh
I would then utter, before
dingdonging and mooing my way
through all the lexicons and languages
of imprecision.

NO NOMINALIST

I'll say a sunshiny thing
and breed grasshoppers in any
grass there is, to rollick there,
playing their green fiddles. Or
I'll say a moonshiny thing and
fish will curl in the glass wall
of any wave going by: you'll smile
at their bright commas. Or I'll say
a rainy thing and snails
will shine on walls under
their cocklehats, peaceful pilgrims
without staffs.

All this so that I won't say
a saying thing, that would uncurtain
a world too real, of
grasshoppers, fishes, snails and
me, grinning all round
at such inventions and frightened
to name you in their midst — I'll not
be Adam and name them, or you,
in case I anger
the friendly archangel and
learn the meaning
of the snake's hiss.

NO CONSOLATION

I consoled myself for not being able to describe
water trickling down a wall or
a wall being trickled down by water
by reflecting that I can see
these two things are not the same thing:
which is more than a wall can do,
or water.
        — But how hard it is
to live at a remove
from a common wall, that keeps out and
keeps in, and from water, that
saves you and drowns you.

But when I went on to notice
that I could see the pair of them
as a trickling wall or as a wall
of water,
it became clear that I can describe only
my own inventions.
        — And how odd to suppose
you prove you love your wife
by continually committing adultery
with her.

WAITING TO NOTICE

I sprawl among seapinks — a statue
fallen from the ruins
of the air into
the twentieth century — and think:
a crowd of fancies is not so easily come by
as you suppose. They have to happen
like weather, or a migration, or a haystack
going up in flames all on its own
half way through some time or other.
When they happen, the mind alerts itself —
it's as if this landscape were suddenly
to become aware
of the existence of its own elements —
possessive rock, possessing
only itself: huge lumbering sea —
that fat-fingered lacemaker who,
by sitting on shells, gives them
their shapes: mountains
reaching half way to somewhere or other:
the heather and grass and me
and a gull, as usual
tuning his bagpipe
and not going on to the tune.

Things there to be noticed.
It takes a sunshaft
to reveal the motes in the air. I wait
for that weather, that sunshaft
to show in the dark room of my mind
that invisible dancing, that
wayward and ceaseless activity, and I bend
my stone arm up till the hawk
hovering over the hayfield
perches fluttering
on my wrist.

Poems from
RINGS ON A TREE

ANTIQUE SHOP WINDOW

Spearsman of molasses, shepherdess
cut from a sugarblock, rings with
varicose stones — all
on a one-legged table perched
on a birdclaw.

And your face in the glass and
my face in the glass, and the real world
behind us translated before us
into dim images, there
— so that the spearsman crouches
on a bird-legged table in
a busy street and the shepherdess runs
through head after head after head
and who can tell
if your face is haunted by the world
or the world by your face?

Look left at the birds stitched
still in their singing, at the sword
half drawn from the scabbard — look left,
more left, to me, this side of the window,
a two-legged, man-legged cabinet
of antique feelings, all of them
genuine.

VISITING HOUR

The hospital smell
combs my nostrils
as they go bobbing along
green and yellow corridors.

What seems a corpse
is trundled into a lift and vanishes
heavenward.

I will not feel, I will not
feel, until
I have to.

Nurses walk lightly, swiftly,
here and up and down and there,
their slender waists miraculously
carrying their burden
of so much pain, so
many deaths, their eyes
still clear after
so many farewells.

Ward 7. She lies
in a white cave of forgetfulness.
A withered hand
trembles on its stalk. Eyes move
behind eyelids too heavy
to raise. Into an arm wasted
of colour a glass fang is fixed,
not guzzling but giving.
And between her and me
distance shrinks till there is none left
but the distance of pain that neither she nor I
can cross.

She smiles a little at this
black figure in her white cave
who clumsily rises
in the round swimming waves of a bell
and dizzily goes off, growing fainter,
not smaller, leaving behind only
books that will not be read
and fruitless fruits.

HOTEL ROOM, 12TH FLOOR

This morning I watched from here
a helicopter skirting like a damaged insect
the Empire State Building, that
jumbo size dentist's drill, and landing
on the roof of the PanAm skyscraper.
But now midnight has come in
from foreign places. Its uncivilised darkness
is shot at by a million lit windows, all
ups and acrosses.

But midnight is not
so easily defeated. I lie in bed, between
a radio and a television set, and hear
the wildest of warwhoops continually ululating through
the glittering canyons and gulches —
police cars and ambulances racing
to the broken bones, the harsh screaming
from coldwater flats, the blood
glazed on sidewalks.

The frontier is never
somewhere else. And no stockades
can keep the midnight out.

LAST NIGHT IN NEW YORK

A fortnight is long enough
to live on a roller-coaster.
Princes Street, Edinburgh, even in the most rushed
of rush hours, you will be
a glade in a wood, I'll wrap myself
in your cool rusticity, I'll
foretell the weather, I'll be
a hick in the sticks.

The sun goes up on Edinburgh.
Manhattan goes up on the sun.
Her buildings overtop Arthur's Seat
and are out of date as soon as
a newspaper. Last year's artist is
a caveman. Tomorrow's best seller
has still to be born.

I plunge through constellations
and basements. My brain spins up there,
I pass it on its way down. I can't see
for the skyscraper in my eye, there's a traffic jam
in my ears. My hands are tacky
with steering my bolting self
through unlikelihoods and impossibilities.
Flags and circuses orbit
my head, I am haloed but not saintly —
poor Faust in 42nd Street.
The tugs in the East River butt
rafts of freight trucks through
my veins. I look at my watch
and its face is Times Square
glittering and crawling with invitations.

Two weeks on a roller-coaster
is long enough. I remember
all islands are not called Coney.

I think, Tomorrow my head will be
higher than my feet, my brain
will come home, I'll be able
to catch up on myself — and, tilting my halo,
I walk out into
exploding precincts and street-bursts.

TRUTH FOR COMFORT

So much effect, and yet so much a cause —
Where things crowd close she is a space to be in:
And makes a marvel where a nowhere was.

Now she's not here I make this nowhere one
That's her effect and it becomes a marvel
To be more marvellous when her journey's done.

Ideas can perch on a nerve and sing.
I listen to their singing and discover
That she can share herself with everything.

This chair, this jug, this picture speak as her,
If in a muted way. Is that so crazy?
My singing mind says No, and I concur.

And is this lies for comfort? She won't know
(Who could not be the cause of lies), for comfort's
What I won't need, until she has to go.

NOW AND FOR EVER

I watch seven sails going in seven directions —
but all heeled over one way.
This satisfies
the dying Calvinist in me,
who is corrupt enough, anyway,
to observe that, if you can't escape
the wrath of God, you can't escape His pleasure
either.

(I remember this morning,
when a marmalade cat made a small rainbow of itself
whose crock of gold was
a rabbit in a bracken bush.
I walked away
from the thin screaming, I couldn't stand
the decorum of that death.)

I dribble through my fingers
what was a rock once
and in my little doomsday
look with unreturned love at a cloud,
at the sea, at a rock where
a cormorant, wings half spread, stands
like a man proving to his tailor
how badly his suit fits.

SLEEPING COMPARTMENT

I don't like this, being carried sideways
through the night. I feel wrong and helpless — like
a timber broadside in a fast stream.

Such a way of moving may suit
that odd snake the sidewinder
in Arizona: but not me in Perthshire.

I feel at rightangles to everything,
a crossgrain in existence. — It scrapes
the top of my head, my footsoles.

To forget outside is no help either —
then I become a blockage
in the long gut of the train.

I try to think I am a through-the-looking-glass
mountaineer bivouacked
on a ledge five feet high.

It's no good. I go sidelong.
I rock sideways . . . I draw in my feet
to let Aviemore pass.

PAINTING—'THE BLUE JAR'

The blue jar jumps forward,
thrust into the room
by the colours round about it.

I wonder,
since it's thrust forward,
what true thing lies
in the fictitious space
behind it.

I sink into my surroundings,
leaving in front of me a fictitious space
where I can be invented.

But the blur jar helplessly
presents itself. It holds out a truth
on a fiction. It keeps its place
by being out of it.

I admire the muscles of pigments
that can hold out a jar for years
without trembling.

ORGY

Thinking of painters, musicians, poets,
who visited the world outside them and the world
inside them and brought back
their sweet discoveries, only to be devoured
by those they brought them to,
I remembered
a wood near Queensferry, where
a banquet of honeydew, that sweet exudation,
was spread on a million airy leaf-tables
in an avenue of lime trees.

Under the tables,
on the broad path below,
a million bees crawled and fell about,
blind drunk.

And a million ants
bit into their soft bellies
for the intoxicating liquor stored
in these tiny tuns — having discovered
that the innkeeper was the inn.

RHU MOR

Gannets fall like the heads of tridents,
bombarding the green silk water
off Rhu Mor. A salt seabeast of a timber
pushes its long snout
up on the sand, where a seal,
struggling in the straitwaistcoat of its own skin,
violently shuffles towards the frayed wave,
the spinning sandgrains, the
caves of green.

I sit in the dunes — the wind
has moulded the sand in pastry frills
and cornices: flights of grass
are stuck in it — their smooth shafts shiver
with trickling drops of light.

Space opens and from the heart of the matter
sheds a descending grace that makes,
for a moment, that naked thing, being,
a thing to understand.

I look out from it
at the grave and simple elements
gathered round a barrage of gannets
whose detonations
explode the green into white.

BROOKLYN COP

Built like a gorilla but less timid,
thick-fleshed, steak-coloured, with two
hieroglyphs in his face that mean
trouble, he walks the sidewalk and the
thin tissue over violence. This morning
when he said, "See you, babe" to his wife,
he hoped it, he truly hoped it.
He is a gorilla
to whom "Hiya, honey" is no cliché.

Should the tissue tear, should he plunge through
into violence, what clubbings, what
gunshots between Phoebe's
Whamburger and Louie's Place.

Who would be him, gorilla with a nightstick,
whose home is a place
he might, this time, never get back to?

And who would be who have to be
his victims?

NAMES

In that shallow water
swim extraordinary little fish
with extraordinary names
they don't know they've been given —
rock goby, lumpsucker, father lasher.   .

I sit among sea lavender and see it. Easy
to point and say buckthorn,
tamarisk, purple rocket.
But they no more know these names
than I know who named them.

I know your name and who named you.
But you have selves as secret from me
as blenny or butterfish.
I sit by you and see you
with eyes ignorant as a glasswort
and I name you and name you
and wonder how it is
that the weight of your name, the most ponderable
thing I know, should raise
my thoughts up
from one shallow pool to
another where
we move always sideways to each other, like
a velvet fiddler and a porcelain crab.

THRESHING

The corn stack dwindles in
The wintry air. Jess,
The terrier, has killed twenty
Rats and looks for more . . .
He heaps chaff in a hill;
His eyes are red and sore.

They see him as he was
Twenty years ago,
Ruddy and tall and glowing,
Filled with his natural Spring —
Full of grace as a cornstalk,
His fat seed ripening.

Time clanks and smokes in the thin
And wintry air. He sees
The stack fall in and easy
Straws lying all about
While chaff heaps up in a hill
And hidden rats run out.

ESTUARY

Saltings and eelgrass
and mud dimpling under the moon —
a place for curlews but not for me; a place
for dunlin, godwit, sandpiper, turnstone
but not for me.

The light is blue. The far away tide
shines like a fish in a cupboard.

I see the blues of your eyes.

Don't step on the little green crab.
Don't step on the mud hump, it will hold you
in a soft fist.

Your brow shines. The inside
of a mussel shell shines. I make
horrible correspondences.

Somewhere behind us
a clear river has died, its muscles
gone slack, its innumerable voices turned
into sounds of sucking and slithering.

Can we turn back? Let me take
your hand, cold as eelgrass, and look for
a meadow furred with fresh water, let me
turn the blues of your eyes away
from the moon dimpling in mud.

By correspondence then
your eyes will be clear, you will
sometimes look at me, you will laugh
at the lolloping hare or the hedgehog trundling by
like a mediaeval siege engine — at a world
of beginnings, at a world of possibly
desperate ends, but
a world of beginnings.

Poems from
A MAN IN MY POSITION

THE ROOT OF IT

On the rug by the fire
a stack of vocabulary rose up, confidently
piling adjectives and nouns and
tiny muscular verbs, storey by storey,
till they reached
almost to the ceiling. The word at the bottom
was love.

I rushed from the room. I
did not believe it. Feverishly
I turned over the pages of the dictionary
to find the blank spaces
they had left behind them — and there they were,
terrible as eyesockets.

What am I to do? What
am I to do? For I know
that tall stack would collapse,
every word would fly back and fill
those terrible spaces,
if I could snatch that word
from the bottom of the pile — if
I could learn again
the meaning of love.

SO MANY SUMMERS

Beside one loch, a hind's neat skeleton,
Beside another, a boat pulled high and dry:
Two neat geometries drawn in the weather:
Two things already dead and still to die.

I passed them every summer, rod in hand,
Skirting the bright blue or the spitting gray,
And, every summer, saw how the bleached timbers
Gaped wider and the neat ribs fell away.

Time adds one malice to another one —
Now you'd look very close before you knew
If it's the boat that ran, the hind went sailing.
So many summers, and I have lived them too.

NO END, NO BEGINNING

I

... And a moon fat as a butterball
Over the wet feathers of treetops;
Meadowsweet smelling of gray honey;
The sealoch bulged like a biceps
In a jersey sleeve of rocks ...
When ever was there a beginning? —
Not of night and its furniture,
Its transcriptions, its cool décor;
Nor of thinking about it:
But when was there a beginning
Of this turbulent love
For a sea shaking with light
And lullabying ditchwater
And a young twig being grave
Against constellations — these —
And people, invisibly webbing
Countries and continents,
Weeping, laughing, being idle
And always, always
Moving from light to darkness and
To light: a furniture
Of what? — a transcription, a décor
Of Being, that hard abstract
Curled in the jelly of an eye
And webbed through constellations
And cities and deserts, and frayed
In the wet feathers of treetops.

2

On the track to Fewin I met
heaped hills — a still-life of enormous apples:
and an owl swivelling his face like a plate
in a fir tree: and a grassgreen beetle
like a walking brooch.
All themselves and all likenesses.

Or I peer down from a sea rock
through the sidling glass, the salty light,
and see in that downward world green Samoas
and swaying Ceylons.

Resemblance makes kinships. Your face,
girl in my mind, is the heir
of all the beautiful women there have been.
I look and dazzle with the loveliness
of women I've never known.

Such a web of likenesses. No matter
how many times removed, I am cousin
to volcanoes and leafbuds, and the heron
devouring a frog eats a bloodbrother of
suns and gravestones.

3

When you, in your unimaginable self,
suddenly were there, shut boxes opened

and worlds flew out coloured like picture books
and full of heavy lethargies and gay dances:

when I met a tree, my old familiar, I knew
this was the first time I was meeting it;

and the birds in it singing — for the first time
I could crack the code of their jargon.

And the boredom and loneliness
in the lit rooms of monotonous streets became

terrible and pitiful — you made me a member
of the secret society of humanity.

The future that had been failing muscles,
sagging flesh, cindering eyes —

all mine, all only mine — swarmed in the air
and spread its new meaning back

into every yesterday. Flux, revolution
emerged into sense, into their own

explanations. I could understand them,
not wholly, but I could understand them

as I could know, not wholly, the meaning
of your still hand, quiet look, a way of walking

that takes you from the first garden to the future
where the apple hangs, still, on its dangerous tree.

4

The dinghy across the bay
Puts out two hands and swims
An elegant backstroke over
A depth full of images.

A gull swings round a rock,
Glides by. No feathers stir —
Dead still as a living fossil
In a geology of air.

I pick a round grassblade
And chew it. The sap breeds
A campfire, dark figures, a blackness
Full of dangerous woods.

And in that tree, that house,
That girl on the gray rocks,
That wave — in everything
A vigorous future kicks.

He'll be born, full of graves,
Greedy and angry. His screams
Will fill us with an ancient pity.
He'll lie helpless in our arms.

115

BASKING SHARK

To stub an oar on a rock where none should be,
To have it rise with a slounge out of the sea
Is a thing that happened once (too often) to me.

But not too often — though enough. I count as gain
That once I met, on a sea tin-tacked with rain,
That roomsized monster with a matchbox brain.

He displaced more than water. He shoggled me
Centuries back — this decadent townee
Shook on a wrong branch of his family tree.

Swish up the dirt and, when it settles, a spring
Is all the clearer. I saw me, in one fling,
Emerging from the slime of everything.

So who's the monster? The thought made me grow pale
For twenty seconds while, sail after sail,
The tall fin slid away and then the tail.

GREEN STAIN

A filth of leaves, she said, a froth, she said
Of sudsy flowers, and there's your mawkish Spring.
Oh, barebone tree, what has it done to you?
Black field, you're gone but for remembering.

I keep my winter where my heart should be.
— I'd rather bear it in its blackest moods
Than see those frilly leaves and blossoms make
A haberdashery of wholesome woods.

A mish-mash green, a sickly groping, such
A fumbling into light! How could they surpass
The icy shapes of darling winter hidden
In luckless trees and ill-starred meadow grass?

WILD OATS

Every day I see from my window
pigeons, up on a roof ledge — the males
are wobbling gyroscopes of lust.

Last week a stranger joined them, a snowwhite
pouting fantail,
Mae West in the Women's Guild.
What becks, what croo-croos, what
demented pirouetting, what a lack
of moustaches to stroke.

The females — no need to be one of them
to know
exactly what they were thinking — pretended
she wasn't there
and went dowdily on with whatever
pigeons do when they're knitting.

ONE OF THE MANY DAYS

I never saw more frogs
than once at the back of Ben Dorain.
Joseph-coated, they ambled and jumped
in the sweet marsh grass
like coloured ideas.

The river ran glass in the sun.
I waded in the jocular water
of Loch Lyon. A parcel of hinds
gave the V-sign with their ears, then
ran off and off till they were
cantering crumbs. I watched
a whole long day
release its miracles.

But clearest of all I remember
the Joseph-coated frogs
amiably ambling or
jumping into the air — like
coloured ideas
tinily considering
the huge concept of Ben Dorain.

A MAN IN MY POSITION

Hear my words carefully.
Some are spoken
not by me, but
by a man in my position.

What right has he
to use my mouth? I hate him
when he touches you
the wrong way.

Yet he loves you also,
this appalling stranger
who makes windows of my eyes.
You see him looking out.

Until he dies
of my love for you
hear my words carefully —
for who is talking now?

STRUCTURES

Stand in this shade and think of me as me —
The moon's a pedant of the present tense
And I'm recessions, my own short history.

I changed before you changed me, as you must
Be differences in this moment's mode:
Stars once were gases or exploding dust.

I'm no forever. My tomorrow's man,
Necrophilous of me, will all the same
Have bridged a crack that only I could span.

I'll grin with new jaws in your smiling face,
That dulcet resurrection, but not forget
The one I now see in this moment's place.

Don't tie me down in it. Recession has
Its gifts to give, though some of them to guess —
Being differences hard for logic, as

The great world leader was a schoolboy dunce,
A sandgrain was a hilltop and — look up —
That moon's blood orange was a cat's claw once.

VENUS FLY-TRAP

Ridding my mind of cant
With one deft twist of my most deep convictions,
I find you are less animal than plant.

You suck the rank soil in
And flourish, on your native commonplaces,
The lively signal of a sense of sin.

I buzzed and landed, but,
Encroaching with my loving bumbling fumble,
Found the whole world go black. The trap was shut.

Now in your juices, I
Am helpless to give warning to my rivals
And, worse, have to digest them when they die.

And worst, since now I'm one
Of your true converts, what is all my labour? —
To flaunt your signals in the shocking sun.

SHIFTS

I walked you away from three corners.
Why do you want to feel trapped?
When I ask you why you pretend love is cruel,
you say, In case it is.

I walk you into a cornerless place
and say, Look, if there's nowhere to run to,
there's nothing to run from. But you stare wildly
    around
and run and run till you come
to that fourth corner, and from it
you beckon me, smiling
at last with love. Do you pretend
I'm your trapper, your hunter,
in case I am?

Be careful. These shifts
so tire me out I wonder
if I'm only pretending to love you
·in case I do.

WALKING TO INVERUPLAN

Glowing with answers in the aromatic dark,
I walk, so wise,
Under the final problem of lit skies.

I reach the bridge, where the road turns north to Stoer,
And there perch me
Under the final problem of a tree.

I'm in my Li Po mood. I've half a mind
To sit and drink
Until the moon, that's just arisen, should sink.

The whisky's good, it constellates. How wise
Can a man be,
I think, inside that final problem, me.

If you are short of answers, I've got them all
As clear as day . . .
I blink at the moon and put the bottle away

And then walk on (for there are miles to go
And friends to meet)
Above the final problem of my feet.

SPILLED SALT

A salt hill
the size it is
because I'm the size I am.

Suilven (that mountain)
since it notices nothing
takes its size from me . . .

That grief I suffered
when she died
was made to my measure.

I loved her, I mourned her
with all the love I had,
with all the grief I had.

She whose look
gave me the size
I thought I was

became spilled salt;
for she
had stopped noticing.

I look at her image
I hate it.
I sweep it away.

IN MY MIND

I go back ways to hurl rooftops
into that furze-blazing sunset.

I stare at water
frilling a stone, flexing a muscle.

Down sidestreets I sniff
cats in passages, old soup and

in one hot room
the fierce smell of hyacinths.

From the tops of spires
I lasso two counties in an eye-blink

and break my ears with a jukebox
in a frowsy cellar.

I am an honorary citizen
of these landscapes and a City Father

of this city. I walk
through its walls and burn

as traffic lights. It is all
lines on my hand.

But I turn away
from that terrible cul-de-sac.

I turn away from
the smiling house there

and the room in it
with green blinds drawn

and a bed with a bed lamp shedding
its kind light down

on a dead hand
and a book fallen from it.

Poems from
THE WHITE BIRD

STAGES

The wave's grip loosened and it fell
off the rock, leaving in cracks and crevices
snuffling sponges of yellow froth.

I sat on stones that had been taken
from a derelict house to patch
a house now derelict.

Through its staved walls I could see
the wrecks of objects that had been made
from the wrecks of ships.

It made me boast of me,
not quite derelict, not quite a wreck, not yet
lodged in a cosy crevice.

I walked off, striking my foot
against a rotten sheep crook, tied down
and left to die in Lilliput.

BOOKWORM

I open the second volume
of a rose
and find it says, word for word,
the same as the first one.

The waves of the sea
annoy me, they bore me;
why aren't they divided
in paragraphs?

I look at the night
and make nothing of it —
those black pages
with no print.

But I love the gothic script
of pinetrees and
on the pond the light's
fancy italics.

And the cherry tree's petals —
they make
a sweet lyric, I appreciate
their dying fall.

But it's strange, girl, how I come back
from the library of everything
to stare and stare at
the closed book of you.

When will you open to me
and show me the meaning of all
the hard words
in the lexicon of love?

AFTER HIS DEATH

It turned out
that the bombs he had thrown
raised buildings:

that the acid he had sprayed
had painfully opened
the eyes of the blind.

Fishermen hauled
prizewinning fish
from the water he had polluted.

We sat with astonishment
enjoying the shade
of the vicious words he had planted.

The government decreed that
on the anniversary of his birth
the people should observe
two minutes pandemonium.

WORDS IN NOWHERE

With you not here what have I not to say?
I beat my mind dazed on the space between us.
— I'd write you; but the words have gone away.

The words gone? No: they bulge so in my net
I can't haul them up from the great depth between us
No matter how the stretched ropes fray and fret.

And my mind, rejecting limits as it must do,
Mindlessly rages through the time between us
In search of the where and when that make up you.

Yet all this shows, when all's not said or done,
That what's between us is all that's between us —
Our single quarrel that proves that we have none.

OLD MAPS AND NEW

There are spaces
where infringements are possible.
There are notices that say:
Trespassers will be welcome.

Pity leaks through the roof
of the Labour Exchange.
In the Leader's pocket,
wrapped in the plans for the great offensive,
are sweets for the children
and a crumpled letter.

There are spaces still to be filled
before the map is completed —
though these days it's only
in the explored territories
that men write, sadly,
Here live monsters.

DUDE

With goldmines in each corner,
Halcyons making ridiculous all my seas,
    Breakfasts with angels, cruises
    Through laughing Hesperides;

    One season, and it all summer,
And doom with a wreath of flowers to dance for me,
    With suns on my rubied fingers,
    Stars gartered below each knee;

    I giggle my tall love for you,
I stilt my praises, bow with a wooing grace
    And have no word of mourning
    To shade your turning face,

    But, glass of your smiling fashion,
Saunter in bliss and, quizzing the natives there,
    Discover them all your subjects
    With gold straws in their hair.

SPARROW

He's no artist.
His taste in clothes is more
dowdy than gaudy.
And his nest — that blackbird, writing
pretty scrolls on the air with the gold nib of his beak,
would call it a slum.

To stalk solitary on lawns,
to sing solitary in midnight trees,
to glide solitary over gray Atlantics —
not for him: he'd rather
a punch-up in a gutter.

He carries what learning he has
lightly — it is, in fact, based only
on the usefulness whose result
is survival. A proletarian bird.
No scholar.

But when winter soft-shoes in
and these other birds —
ballet dancers, musicians, architects —
die in the snow
and freeze to branches,
watch him happily flying
on the O-levels and A-levels
of the air.

MIRROR TALK

In such falsities, she said,
I recognise your loving truth.
I hated her for it.

When you stay away, she said,
I forgive you, for I know
you're longing to come back.
I hated her for that, too.

When you hurt me, she said,
I know you're hurting not me
but the world.
Pretentious fool.

I can't leave her
for I secretly know
she knows she is lying.
This adds her hurt
to my guilt.

How can so helpless a thing as truth
survive
so many wounds?

MOMENT MUSICAL IN ASSYNT

A mountain is a sort of music: theme
And counter theme displaced in air amongst
Their own variations.
Wagnerian Devil signed the Coigach score;
And God was Mozart when he wrote Cul Mor.

You climb a trio when you climb Cul Beag.
Stac Polly — there's a rondo in seven sharps,
Neat as a trivet.
And Quinag, rallentando in the haze,
Is one long tune extending phrase by phrase.

I listen with my eyes and see through that
Mellifluous din of shapes my masterpiece
Of masterpieces:
One sandstone chord that holds up time in space —
Sforzando Suilven reared on his ground bass.

THE LITTLE FALLS POOL

Giggle and thump —
the water does both at once.
The stone it creases over
smiles like a mandarin,
porcelained with water.
Upstream, a posse
of baby mergansers
squatters, eight squeaks in a line,
across a sliding prairie of water.
It all makes happiness
seem easy.

There's a cloud
in the space between us.
Cruelty roams there,
cruelty and desolation.
There are sad minds
in the space between us
(and happiness, and happiness).
But where you are
and where I am
there is room only
for happiness natural as this water
creased over a stone. I watch
the eight fluff-balls running on its surface
with love, knowing they'll reach
the dark overhang
where their mother waits for them.

COLD SONG

The doctor gazed
at the sack of guts passing
and saw
my pretty girl.

The lawyer looked at
a ringless finger
and saw my
pretty girl.

The professor noticed
eyes quick with intelligence
and
saw my pretty girl.

I met my pretty girl
and saw an intelligent
sack of guts with
a ringless finger.

NEW TABLES

A mathematician who came to his senses
thought deeply
(putting his finger to his forehead,
putting his finger through his forehead)
and wrote:

One robust curse equals
two shrieks, four groans:
One hour with you
equals every convalescence:
One boy on a scooter equals
transport:
One Yes equals ten
commandments:
One new life equals
a million old deaths:
Love equals
equal.

The world read this, stupefied
with admiration
and went on dying and laughing
and shedding
logarithms of tears.

COUNTRY DANCE

The room whirled and coloured
and figured itself with dancers.
Another gaiety seemed born of theirs
and flew like streamers
between their heads and the ceiling.

I gazed, coloured and figured,
down the tunnel of streamers —
and there, in the band, an old fiddler
sawing away in the privacy
of music. He bowed lefthanded and his right hand
was the wrong way round. Impossible.
But the jig bounced, the gracenotes
sparkled on the surface of the tune.
The odd man out, when it came to music,
was the odd man in.

There's a lesson here, I thought, climbing
into the pulpit I keep in my mind.
But before I'd said Firstly brethren, the tune
ended, the dancers parted, the old fiddler
took a cigarette from the pianist, stripped off
the paper and ate the tobacco.

TREE HUNG WITH FAIRY LIGHTS

It's not additions but extensions give
A thing its further self,
Changed from within:
Blossom's a sort of leaf, as nail is skin.

But decoration contradicts the tree.
I love you best (and know
It's love, not lust)
When clothed in nothing but your altered dust.

DOWN AND DOWN

Therefore I fall
in a way that never misses the target
like all the marvellous fallers
Icarus Phaethon (Lucifer).

The depth I fall into
is cruelly just light enough
for me to see it;
else how know I was falling?

I had only the usual
pride, the usual ambition.
Icarus Phaethon Lucifer,
I will be no legend.

When I reach the bottom
of bottomlessness, there will be
no broken wings beside me,
no chariot of the sun.

And no crystal battlements
will infinitely shine above me.
I will be left with only
the loneliness of falling.

IN A MIST

The mountains fold and move.
I'm not quite lost. The thing that troubles me
Is that the easiest way out
Is not the one that's easiest to see.

I know just where you are.
But how to get there when lochs change their place
And the familiar track
Squirms like an adder into the heather bushes?

I curse my senses: and speak
Into the mist: Stay where you are, please stay —
I've got my compass yet.
It'll get me to you, if not by the easiest way.

Poems from
THE WORLD'S ROOM

RETURN TO SCALPAY

The ferry wades across the kyle. I drive
The car ashore
On to a trim tarred road. A car on Scalpay?
Yes, and a road where never was one before.
The ferrymen's Gaelic wonders who I am
(Not knowing I know it) this man back from the dead,
Who takes the blue-black road (no traffic jam)
From by Craig Lexie over to Bay Head.

A man bows in the North wind, shaping up
His lazybeds,
And through the salt air vagrant peat smells waver
From houses where no house should be. The sheds
At the curing station have been newly tarred.
Aunt Julia's house has vanished. The Red Well
Has been bulldozed away. But sharp and hard
The church still stands, barring the road to Hell.

A chugging prawn boat slides round Cuddy Point
Where in a gale
I spread my batwing jacket and jumped farther
Then I've jumped since. There's where I used to sail
Boats looped from rushes. On the jetty there
I caught eels, cut their heads off and watched them slew
Slow through the water. Ah — Cape Finisterre
I called that point, to show how much I knew.

While Hamish sketches, a crofter tells me that
The Scalpay folk,
Though very intelligent, are not Spinozas. . .
We walk the Out End road (no need to invoke
That troublemaker, Memory, she's everywhere)
To Laggandoan, greeted all the way —
My city eyeballs prickle; it's hard to bear
With such affection and such gaiety.

Scalpay revisited? — more than Scalpay. I
Have no defence,
For half my thought and half my blood is Scalpay,
Against that pure, hardheaded innocence
That shows love without shame, weeps without shame,
Whose every thought is hospitality —
Edinburgh, Edinburgh, you're dark years away.

Scuttering snowflakes riddling the hard wind
Are almost spent
When we reach Johann's house. She fills the doorway,
Sixty years of size and astonishment,
Then laughs and cries and laughs, as she always did
And will (Easy glum, easy glow, a friend would say) . . .
Scones, oatcakes, herrings from under a bubbling lid.
Then she comes with us to put us on our way.

Hugging my arm in her stronger one, she says,
Fancy me
Walking this road beside my darling Norman!
And what is there to say? . . . We look back and see
Her monumental against the flying sky
And I am filled with love and praise and shame
Knowing that I have been, and knowing why,
Diminished and enlarged. Are they the same?

They sprint eight feet and —
stop. Like that. They
sprintayard (like that) and
stop.
They have no acceleration
and no brakes.
Top speed's their only one.

They're alive — put life
through a burning-glass, they're
its focus — but they share
the world of delicate clockwork.

In spasmodic
Indian file
they parallel the parallel ripples.

When they stop
they, suddenly, are
gravel.

PROGRESS

That was the beginning
of an idea — what isn't
the beginning of an idea?

Frog spawn glowed
in the ponds in the thickets
and a melancholy hooter made
mastodon noises over the city.
Everything was as usual.

Then the idea became
a myth — a thing
that ought to be stopped.

And ships sidled uneasily
beside hairy wharfs and in a lighted room
someone cried out with love. Everything
was as usual.

And the myth in the idea grew teeth
and iron wings. It clanked
through the air over
its flat shadow.

And legs arms heads were buried
in the rubble of cities. Great minds
rotted black. And everything
was as usual, everything wept beside
an endless column of refugees.
And good minds said No, good minds
kept saying No. And the word
created a silence round it
and was heard by no-one.

GREENSHANK

His single note — one can't help calling it
piping, one can't help
calling it plaintive — slides droopingly down
no more than a semitone, but is filled
with an octave of loneliness, with the whole sad scale
of desolation.

He won't leave us. He keeps flying
fifty yards and perching
on a rock or a small hummock,
drawing attention to himself.
Then he calls and calls
and flies on again
in a flight
roundshouldered but dashing,
skulking yet bold.

Cuckoo, phoenix, nightingale,
you are no truer emblems
than this bird is.
He is the melancholy that flies
in the weathers of my mind,
He is the loneliness that calls to me there
in a semitone
of desolate octaves.

HOROSCOPE

I know there are words I don't understand
like apogee and azimuth.
I know there are diagrams that pretend to be
diagrams of the past and gossips
of the future.

It's my pretty Now I'm in love with
that won't stand still
to be measured. The past
has gone to a far country; and as for the future
there's no future in it.
But my pretty Now, I love her, I love her,
because she shows herself off to me
and will always be faithful.

IN A WHIRL

The cross-migrations going on in my mind!
I'm dizzied blind
And blinded dizzy by those pantomime
And stroboscopic scene-shiftings. Old Time
Rattles his knees and, grinning fit to kill,
Jigs at all angles in the astounded air.
What can I do but stare
And carol won't you, will you, won't you, Will?

An Immanence is what I want, to be
That Unity
That transcendantal One I don't believe in.
How give it birth with no place to conceive in? —
My brain cells all are full: their prisoners lie,
Far too contented, on their bunks and grin
Even though I smuggle in
Files and ropeladders in the proper pie.

There was a time Time kept his printed place
In lower case.
But now he's boss and bully and off his head.
He's displaced place and promoted from the dead
His grandpa Chaos — it's terrifying to see
The douce Laws capering in hippy gear:
A jingbang where it's clear
(Good godless God!) that Immanence is me.

153

GONE ARE THE DAYS

Impossible to call a lamb a lambkin
or say eftsoons or spell you ladye.
My shining armour bleeds when it's scratched;
I blow the nose that's part of my visor.

When I go pricking o'er the plain
I say *Eightpence please* to the sad conductress.
The towering landscape you live in has printed
on its portcullis *Bed and breakfast*.

I don't regret it. There are wildernesses
enough in Rose Street or the Grassmarket
where dragons' breaths are methylated
and social workers trap the unwary.

So don't expect me, lady with no e,
to look at a lamb and feel lambkin
or give me a down look because I bought
my greaves and cuisses at Marks and Spencers.

Pishtushery's out. But oh, how my heart swells
to see you perched, perjink, on a bar stool.
And though epics are shrunk to epigrams, let me
buy a love potion, a gin, a double.

UNDERSTANDING

It was an evening, one of those evenings
when flutes play audibly and God's thrombosis
isn't too sore, and human fingers
touch human fingers in immortal braille.

And there was an O in my graph, though discursions
dangled from anywhere — from brambles or the pretty
armpits of lambs; and a stone was more
than just a thing for a vole to go round.

The praise is yours, girl: for you made
everything braille for my blind fingers.
Everything spoke you; for you are the word
to which all other words are a footnote.

It was an evening, one of the many
when your meaning was all the others'
and love and pity were the O in the graph
of the world's loneliness, of wars, and disasters.

DRIFTING IN A DINGHY

Cloud, light, air, water and its depth —
a treble clef, on which
I am my monotonous single,
black breve
on a shining manuscript.

I think of grammar, I think of you.

— Subject, verb object in one,
your meaning is an everlasting
narrative of illuminations.
Yet I can no more analyse
the syntax of your going or parse
your parts of all speech
than I can explain why music
is a narrative of all illuminations except
yours, even though I can't tell
an organum from
a diminished clavichord.

I hum melodiously
in this abstraction of music,
thinking of grammar, thinking of you,
till a woodwind sighs from the west
and my black breve
goes sharp, goes flat, goes sharp.

THE UNLIKELY AS USUAL

Green in the grass is a blade of grass
But you in my mind are a fiery cluster.
Milky the stars in the Milky Way —
In my dusty thoughts you're glinting gold dust.

Once I glimpsed in my thickety wood
A crimson unicorn. It snorted bluebells
And piaffered violets and like an angel
Vanished, leaving the air true.

On lucky days I visit that truth
And find you walking there, being gentle
With shades and toadstools and toadstool moss.
Each of these times is a lucky again.

A waterdrop is green in its wave
But you in any of the world's spaces
Deny likeness — and yet you make
The law of likeness a state of grace.

Unicorn, what were you in the shades
With your melting eyes and lifted forefoot?
You reached from myth and gave me a girl
Whose like was never in that wood before.

PRIVATE

Those who recognise my mask and recognise
my words — all to be found in the dictionary —
shall I scare them, bore them
with a truth? Shall I distort
the words to be found in the dictionary
in order to say what they mean
when they mean me?

How my friends would turn away
from the ugly sounds coming from my mouth.
How they would grieve for
that comfortable MacCaig whose
small predictions were predictable.
How they would wish back
the clean white bandages
that hid these ugly wounds.

BIRTHDAYS

In the earliest light of a long day
three stags stepped out from the birch wood
at Achmelvich bridge
to graze on the sweet grass
by the burn.
A gentle apparition.

Stone by stone a dam was built,
a small dam, small stone by stone.
And the water backed up, flooding
that small field.

I'll never see it again.
It's drowned forever.
But still
in the latest light of a lucky day I see
horned heads come from the thickets
and three gentle beasts innocently pacing
by that implacable water.

STAG IN A NEGLECTED HAYFIELD

He's not in his blazing red yet. His antlers
Are a foot that'll be a spreading yard.
The field was a hayfield: now a heifer
And two cows graze there and no dog barks.

That's the outward scene. The inner —
A mountain forgotten, a remembered man.
The deer will return to the hill: but stiller
Than the stone above them are the scything hands.